A JOURNEY
THROUGH TEA

A journey through the tea gardens
of Duncan Brothers in Bangladesh and
those of the Goodricke Group in India

PHOTOGRAPHED BY
ELIZABETH HANDY

"Tea tempers the spirits and harmonizes the mind, dispels lassitude and relieves fatigue, awakens thought and prevents drowsiness, lightens up or refreshes the body, and clears the perceptive faculties"

CONFUCIUS 551 — 479 BC

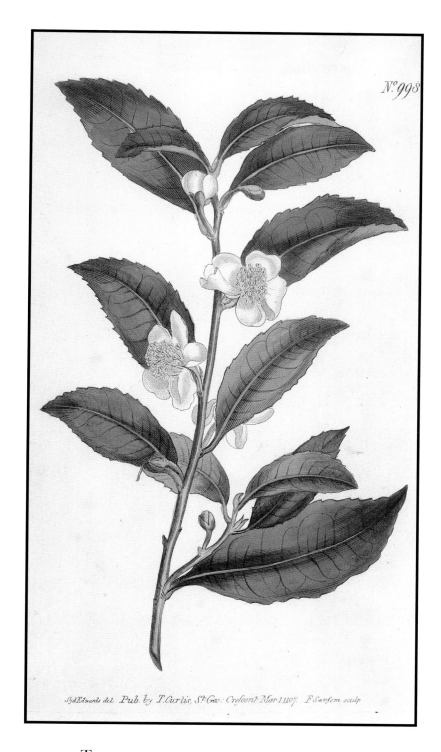

Syd Edwards del. Pub. by T. Curtis, St. Geo: Crescent Mar. 1 1807. F Sansom sculp

THEA CHINENSIS VARIETY B BOHEA TEA-TREE

First Published 1997,
Reprinted 2001

Text © Charles Handy
All new photographs © by Elizabeth Handy
except those acknowledged

ISBN 0 9527549 1 6

Design by Elizabeth Handy
Typesetting by The County Press
Origination, printing and binding in Singapore
under the supervision of Keith Allison of
MRM Graphics Ltd, Winslow, Bucks.

SPONSORED BY LAWRIE GROUP PLC

All of the profits from this book will go to the
Sir Percival Griffiths' Tea Planters Trust
Copies available at £15 (inclusive of postage and packing) from
Lawrie Plantation Services Limited
Tel: 01732 884488
Fax: 01732 885724
e-mail leggatt@lawrieps.co.uk

CONTENTS

CHARLES HANDY AMONGST THE TEA BUSHES AT AIBHEEL TEA GARDEN

PREFACE

BY CHARLES HANDY

CHARLES HANDY IS A MANAGEMENT WRITER, BROADCASTER AND
SOCIAL PHILOSOPHER.

Peter Leggatt amongst the tea bushes at Aibheel Tea Garden

LEARNING FROM TEA

6.00 am. Dawn on Badamtam tea garden near Darjeeling. I stood on the little mound behind the tennis court and looked at the pinkish clouds hovering across the valley, and then, way above them, I saw, floating as if in another world, the majestic peaks of Kanchenjunga, surely one of the queens of mountains. Down below, the camellia bushes of the tea gardens covered the ground like some shiny green tablecloth. It was beautiful, other-worldly and timeless.

I reflected then, because it was a moment for such reflections, of how temporary mankind's creations are when set against the real timelessness of the mountains, and of how the things and the institutions made by man have constantly to change if they are to continue the same, something which is true even of ourselves as persons. For that camellia tablecloth to look the same there has to be regular pruning and replanting. Where once the supervisors went their rounds on ponies, now they used Yamaha motorcycles. The charming bungalow where we were staying once housed the English manager, but now, updated and improved, was home to the Indian manager and his charming family, while the whole estate belonged, today, to a different company than the one which owned it then. What, I wondered, would have to change in the future for the view I saw below me to stay the same?

We, my photographer wife and I, were the privileged guests of the Lawrie Group, invited to visit some of their tea gardens in Bangladesh and India, and were fortunate to do so in the company of the local Chairman, Peter Leggatt. For us, the world of tea was something completely new, and endlessly fascinating. As a social philosopher and student of organizations I was intrigued to find, in those tea gardens of the Indian sub-continent, a ready understanding of the wider responsibilities and purposes of management, topics which are now the subject of much soul-searching among the better businesses of the West. I realised, too, how much we have to learn from the traditions of other cultures, especially those of the East, which often have direct relevance to the way we live and plan our lives.

THE PAST

The Manager's Bungalow, Badamtam Tea Garden, in 1913.

THE MANAGEMENT LESSONS

Because of what they do and where they are, the tea gardens which we saw offered their people a life, rather than just a job. They told us that it took four pruning cycles, or sixteen years, really to understand the management of a tea garden. Not for the tea manager a quickie MBA followed by a highly paid consultancy assignment. Tea is a career, not a stepping stone. For the workers, male and female, tea offers work and a home for the whole family, along with education, health care and, often, some land to grow their own food. Were these things not on offer there would be no workers, because these gardens are often far from anywhere. These tea companies were still one of the few remaining all-inclusive lifetime organizations, for them 'outsourcing', 'flexible labour forces' and 'temporary managers' were foreign concepts. They were communities, as well as businesses, and the difference could be felt as we walked and talked our way around.

The senior managers, as a consequence, had to take a long-term, almost generational, view of their business, if they had any concern for those who worked for them. Tea bushes, and those who tend them and manage them, take a long time to grow and to be productive. We had only to look with our untrained eyes at the shambles of the gardens where the owners had not taken that generational perspective, but had gone for the short-term rewards, to see how they had sacrificed their future for their present, only to find that, of course, that future soon becomes, in its turn, an impoverished present. I realised, once again, that it is not so much the pressure of any stockmarket that produces a short-term outlook but the way the senior managers see their job. Flexibility, I saw, can be great for productivity but, carried too far, it leaves one free of any commitment to anyone else, and that can quickly destroy the future.

THE FUTURE?

The children of tea workers on their way to school at Badamtam Tea Garden in Darjeeling.
Will they grow up to work in the tea gardens, we wondered, or would they
develop new ambitions?

THE CULTURAL LESSONS

Whether one believes in re-incarnation for oneself or not, a culture in which such beliefs are common has a vested interest in making sure that things go on after ones death, and if possible go on even better, because one might be back again to experience them. Such cultures 'think beyond the grave' as good family businesses often do. They are treeplanting cultures, growing things which they may not live to see in their prime, cathedral builders, starting works not to be completed in their lifetime, works worthy of a God. Religions which look for salvation in another world can short-change this world if they are not careful, and atheistic cultures which measure success by personal accumulations of money, power or fame tend to build office blocks not cathedrals. Capitalism without cathedral thinking gets you nowhere in the end. We need, therefore, in the West, to grow a culture that thinks beyond the grave. While I do not, myself, believe in a personal re-incarnation, I do see myself as a necessary link in the long chain of existence. Without me there would not be my children, or, more widely, without me, I like to think, some things would not have happened that should have happened.

The Hindus teach, I gathered there, that one should not despise or ignore the good things of life, but should enjoy all that life has to offer, as long as one does not get enslaved by them. I heard, there, too, the proverb: "if you have two loaves, go sell one and buy a lily – to lift the heart." We could learn from that. There is, we found on our journey, often a joy in the very act of living which shows in the faces of my wife's portraits of many of the people in the gardens, no matter how simply many of them lived. Indeed, the concept of 'enough', was, I felt, well understood by some, the idea that if you define what 'enough' is, then and only then will you know what is more than enough, and so be free, rather than enslaved.

We met one manager, in Bangladesh, who had taken his family to America in search of advancement and riches. He had found a good job and a nice home and schools for his children but, after a few months, had decided to return to the tea gardens because, he said, of the quality of life there, the peace and the sense of community, none of which he had found in America. He would not be nearly as materially rich in Bangladesh, but he would have enough. That concept of 'enough' did not, however, seem to be so well understood in the 'new' India of the cities where the split between the very rich and the very poor was conspicuous, some who clearly had more than enough and many much less than enough. India might do well to learn from itself as well as from the West while it pursues its new economic policies.

AIBHEEL TEA GARDEN – THE DOOARS

THE FORCES OF CHANGE

In Darjeeling they make the tea by the old traditional methods, with machinery carrying long gone British names. You can see the tea going from process to process, often carried, spread or sorted by hand. It is a sympathetic process, almost a romantic one, but clearly expensive. From Darjeeling we went down from the hills to visit a brand new instant tea plant. These machines had Swedish not British names, and were housed in a sort of postmodern cathedral. You could not actually 'see' any of the tea as it went its way through pipes and cylinders and tubes, but could only see the flow charted on something that looked like a circuit diagram on a silicon chip. Postmodern tea, powdered for the modern taste. And the workers? Few, very few, but highly skilled and very marketable. Not there for life, one suspects.

The tea gardens, too, will surely see some changes. Properly caring, the management, these days, provides good schools for all the youngsters on the estates. When they grow up they may not want to work their days plucking the leaves or tending the factories, or, if they do, they will want and demand more pay. One day machines will pick those leaves, not so tenderly, so quietly or so prettily, but quicker and more cheaply. And so those camellia tablecloths will have to have broad paths cut through them to allow machines to go where before only humans trod. To keep their world alive, some things will have to change.

It requires courage to make changes, and courage to accept change. That courage comes from a belief in the essential goodness of what one is doing and from a desire that it should go on being done, even after one has gone, and even at some cost to oneself, in the best possible way. The growing and making of tea seemed to us to be one of those occupations that call forth the best in people, giving meaning to their work and peace to their lives. It is not often that one spends two weeks 'on location' with working folk and comes away excited, refreshed and wanting to go back. We shall not forget the tea gardens, the people we met or the lessons we learnt.

ELIZABETH HANDY: SELF PORTRAIT IN THE FIELD OPPOSITE HER HOME IN NORFOLK

A PHOTOGRAPHIC JOURNEY

BY ELIZABETH HANDY

ELIZABETH HANDY IS A PORTRAIT PHOTOGRAPHER IN LONDON AND NORFOLK.

PETER LEGGATT, Chairman of the Goodricke Group and Lawrie Plantation Services, our host
and travelling companion, with CHARLES HANDY, signing the visitors' book at the home of
DR MAJOR GENERAL and MRS CHAUDHURY in Aibheel. On this journey, we left our mark on
more visitors' books than I could count!

BANGLADESH

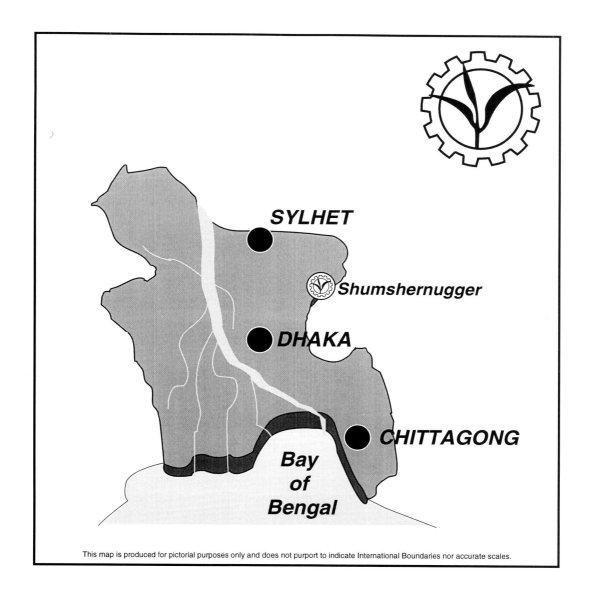

SYLHET

Shumshernugger

DHAKA

CHITTAGONG

Bay
of
Bengal

This map is produced for pictorial purposes only and does not purport to indicate International Boundaries nor accurate scales.

WE STARTED OUR JOURNEY IN BANGLADESH

We travelled upcountry from Dhaka by Range Rover to Shumshernugger Tea Estate,
arriving, at dusk, at Lungla House, the Company Guest House. We did not see the full
beauty of this lovely, and luxurious, place until the following morning. The natural beauty
of the setting and the technological treat of BBC Television in our bedroom
provided a delightful contrast of cultures.

Abu Subhan, Managing Director of Duncan Brothers, Bangladesh

OUR FIRST MORNING

The day begins. Bangladesh is a land of water (sometimes too much of it) and people take full advantage of it.

GREEN VISTAS AND FRIENDLY FACES — MY ABIDING MEMORY OF BANGLADESH

RUBBER NAPPIES?

A rubber plantation in the middle of a tea garden was an unexpected extra, but a useful diversification for a one-product business.

TALK AND TEA

The management of a tea estate is an endlessly fascinating topic. The managers and
their assistants meet to exchange views with Charles, my husband, who was to
discover that the traditions of the East and of Tea had much to offer
the management theorists of the West.

LEFT: MABUD ALI AND RINA

RIGHT: SHAH ALAM AND SHAHEEN

LEFT: 'SHAMS' SHAMSUZZAMAN
AND LUNA

Above: the Manipuri dancer is representing The Lord Krishna

HOSPITALITY — BANGLADESH-STYLE

There always seemed to be some other delicious food to sample, in some other bungalow, with
more welcomes from some of the most elegant women we had met in a long time. The
verandahs of upcountry Bangladesh were more fun than many an English drawing-room.
Where else would one be entertained by the beautiful young
Manipuri dancers and their drummers?

HEALTH IS HAPPINESS, AND PRODUCTIVITY

The Duncan Brothers tea gardens have their own hospitals for their tea workers. MORAG MURDOCH is the administrator of the Camellia Duncan Foundation Hospital which was opened in 1994. Unusually for hospitals, the patients often have to be persuaded to leave this pleasing place.

MORAG MURDOCH

TEA PICKERS

RAJKUMARI RAJBHOR and CHANDRAMA NAIDU picking tea at Lungla tea garden.
The trick is to pick two leaves and a bud in one movement. I tried and failed. These
women do it 50 times a minute! And they make it seem like a ballet movement.
They are paid by results so their dexterity is critical.

THE COMMUNITY

Tea gardens are communities within communities. They have to like one
another if they are to live together.

FATHER JOE LEHANE has a Catholic Mission in Srimangal. He runs a hostel for 20 boys who come from outlying villages in order that they can attend schools. Father Joe might be called an educational entrepreneur — he has started up 37 schools in the area.

Left: Father Joe's first ordinand.

A KHASI VILLAGE GIRL

The Khasi people have their own villages and way of life. They made us very welcome and invited us into their homes, whose cleanliness and tidiness would put most of us to shame. Simplicity, we reflected, may be part of the recipe for contentment.

Ghulam Mustafa the Security Guard at Lungla House.

BY PLANE TO DHAKA

...and a chance to see this rainy but enchanting country from the air.

Right: Bangladeshis take the rain in their stride, treating their floods as an occasional inconvenience even though all they own can often be washed away.

A young man at Shumshernugger

INDIA

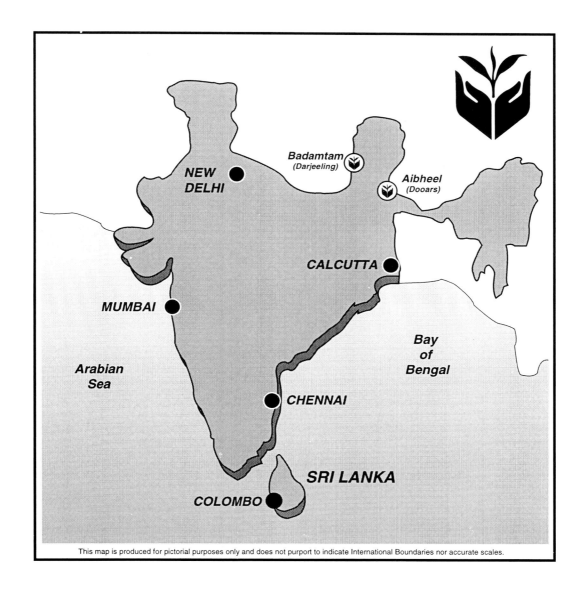

Badamtam
(Darjeeling)

Aibheel
(Dooars)

NEW DELHI

CALCUTTA

MUMBAI

Bay of Bengal

Arabian Sea

CHENNAI

SRI LANKA

COLOMBO

This map is produced for pictorial purposes only and does not purport to indicate International Boundaries nor accurate scales.

CALCUTTA, NEXT STOP

From Dhaka we flew to Calcutta where we stayed at Camellia House as the guest of the Goodricke Group's managing director SATTI BHASIN and his wife SAVITA.

The view from Camellia House, overlooking the Convent for the Sisters of Charity, part of
Mother Teresa's Order. Every morning we watched the Sisters hang out their
laundry, a quiet reminder that religion also has to do with the ordinary things of life!

But there are also extraordinary people, many of them living in Calcutta. We were fortunate to meet two of them — MOTHER TERESA and JYOTI BASU, the Chief Minister, the Saint and the Marxist, but with more in common than one might expect, with their commitment to the poor of that great city.

Above: Badamtam Tea Estate, nestling in the hills below Kanchenjunga.

AND THEN DARJEELING

Darjeeling is home to some of the earliest of the tea plantations, going back 150 years when it
could take two months to make the journey which we had made that day. Then, people
came for five years and not the two nights that we stayed, and some never returned at all.
Reading some of the tales of the early tea planters, we swore that we would
never again complain about the difficulties of life.

And as it was in 1913. The scenery remains the same, but the
reality is very different.

Right: there can be few more beautiful sights in the world than sunrise at Badamtam, as Kanchenjunga pokes its head out of the clouds in the morning light. Tea Gardens are always beautiful, but some have to be more beautiful than others.

Above: the spot from where I took my photograph, as it was in 1913 with the manager Alex Shannon and his wife Lillias.

PROGRESS?

It used to be ponies, now it's a Yamaha. SUBRATA SEN, assistant manager at Badamtam.

BIRESH PAUL, photographer, personal assistant to SATTI BHASIN and, for a few days, an invaluable guide, organizer and friend to us both. He was particularly helpful in enabling me to meet NAR BAHADUR NEWANG (right). NAR BAHADUR has been munshi, or foreman, for five years, and has worked in tea for 36 years.

I also met HOMA SHARMA (right) who is a tea picker. She introduced me to her family in their home (above). KISHEN, her husband, works in the tea factory. BISHNU MAI, Homa's mother lives with them. The children, SUJATA and DEVENDRA, both attend school. Their mother did not go to school.

We met the headmaster MADAN KUMAR SUBBA (right) and the union leader ASHOK MUKHIA (above) when we visited the school at Badamtam for the tea workers' children.

There is no shortage of intellect among the tea workers' children, we thought, looking at the sparkling eyes of the kids.

Badamtam Tea Garden sports day was to be held the following day on the playing fields.
There can't be many playing fields with a better view.

THE DARJEELING CLUB

Nostalgia for the old days oozes out of this place. Even the menu still tastes of an England of yesterday, although not one of the faces now is English. And it has to be the best clubhouse view in the world. The Club is the social centre for many of the Goodricke gardens, and some people drive up to three hours on the twisty mountain roads on club nights.

Menu

L U N C H

Mulligatawny Soup

Grilled Chicken 'N' Garnish

Baked Fish 'N' Dressing

Fish Cutlets

Cold Meat Chicken And Chicken Sausages

Vegetable Cutlets

Baked Mix Vegetable And Dressing

Mixed Boiled Vegetable

Russian Salad

Fruit Crumble

Fruit Salad

The Darjeeling Club Ltd.
Dated..17th..Nov.'95..

****

THE DOOARS — LAST STOP

The Dooars lies below Darjeeling. It is a major tea growing area with many Goodricke gardens.
The roads are bordered by a string of tea gardens, which makes the slow drive over the
potholes not only bearable but a delight for the senses. We stayed as guests of the
Aibheel's tea garden manager, HARI CHOPRA and his wife, RITA (right).

HARI and RITA live in a huge bungalow, where we woke each morning to a visual feast, looking out over a valley of colour. Each evening, RITA provided another kind of feast, to tickle our other senses. It was a hard place to leave.

HARI in his office, where the rollcall of managers changed from
British names to Indian in 1974.

THE OLD, AND THE NOT SO OLD
In many ways, the way of making tea has not changed that much over the
years, although the equipment has (compare the pictures above and right).
Bags not boxes, more conveyor belts and better machines, cleaner premises and concrete
floors instead of wood, and the first fully-automated factory is already up and running.

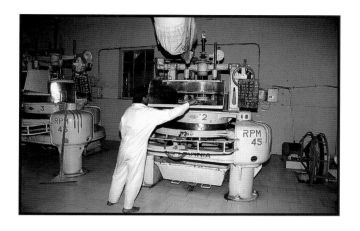

THE VERY NEW

The Instant Tea Plant opened in 1996, at Aibheel, a completely new technology for a very different product, (left) as we saw it, and (above) in its final state.

A new sort of beauty for a new sort of world?

MORE TEA PEOPLE

Faces that we shall remember.

SWAPAN DUTTA, (left) manager of Chulsa tea garden and his wife, (above) KALYANI.

KALU BISWAKARMA, the driver who so skilfully drove us up and
down the twisty and potholed roads.

SURINDER MEHRA, manager of Lakhipara Garden, who hosted us for lunch and where we watched the film *The Queen of the Elephants* made by Mark Shand. This brought home to us the terrible dilemma which tea people face with the elephants. These great and beautiful beasts need the jungle to survive, but the jungle is disappearing as civilization encroaches upon it. Let loose in the tea gardens, the elephants can do terrible damage to property and to people. How can they best preserve both the elephants and the gardens?

DR MAJOR GENERAL SASHI CHAUDHURY, and his wife, SHUVRA, at their bungalow.
General Chaudhury is Chief Medical Officer of the Goodricke Group.

Dr S D Sharma, medical officer, Sathkaya Division.

HOMA SHARMA, a tea picker at Badamtam.

CONCLUSION

We drink tea differently now, back home. We make it carefully, using only what, we now know, is best. We drink it without milk or sugar, to get the purest of its flavours. We realise now, as we never did before, that the thing we make our tea from comes from some of the more beautiful parts of the world, that it started off as a shiny green leaf, growing in what is literally a garden, that it was picked by women like the one opposite, who live and work in a community of tea people, whose work defines their way of life.

We never really understood these things before.

It makes a difference.

We owe a huge debt of gratitude to the LAWRIE GROUP PLC, to DUNCAN BROTHERS BANGLADESH and the GOODRICKE GROUP for giving us this opportunity to learn something about a very special business, one with a colourful history and an exiting future and, above all, to meet some great people of Bangladesh and India.

ACKNOWLEDGEMENTS

Photographs on pages 58, 60 and 71 by Biresh Paul
Photograph on page 32 by permission of Duncan Brothers
All old photographs lent by Mrs Auriol Shannon from her family album.

Maps on pages 19 and 43 drawn by David Hobbs.

Print of Camellia reproduced from *Curtis' Botanical Magazine*
1807 vol 25 plate 998 by permission of The Linnean Society of London.